Strategic Account Strategy

---

version 1.1

Book 1

The Strategic Account Program

Book 2

Planning for Strategic Accounts

Noel Capon

www.axcesscapon.com

Strategic Account Strategy

version 1.1

Book 1

The Strategic Account Program

Book 2

Planning for Strategic Accounts

Noel Capon

R.C. Kopf Professor of International Marketing
Graduate School of Business
Columbia University
New York, NY

W
wessex

Library of Congress Cataloging-in-Publication Data

Capon, Noel
    Strategic Account Strategy / Noel Capon – version 1.1
        p. cm.
    ISBN: 978-0-9833300-1-1
        1. Strategy—Accounts.   I. Title: Strategic Account Strategy.   II. Noel Capon

Editor: Noel Capon
Copy Editor: Christy Goldfinch
Design/Cover Design: Anna Botelho

Dedication

To key, strategic, and

global account managers

who daily strive to deliver

value to their customers and

their own organizations.

ABOUT THE AUTHOR

NOEL CAPON is the R. C. Kopf Professor of International Marketing and past Chair of the Marketing Division at the Graduate School of Business, Columbia University. Professor Capon's early education was in Britain: he holds B.Sc. and Ph.D. degrees from London University – University College. He also holds a Diploma in Business Administration from Manchester Business School, an MBA from Harvard Business School, and a Ph.D. from Columbia University — Columbia Business School.

Professor Capon joined the Columbia Business School faculty in 1979. Previously he was on the faculty of, and received tenure from, the University of California — Graduate School of Management, UCLA. He has taught and held faculty positions at Harvard Business School; Australia — Monash University; England — Bradford Management Centre and Manchester Business School; France — INSEAD; Hong Kong — The Hong Kong University of Science and Technology (HKUST); China — China European International Business School (CEIBS — Shanghai); and India — Indian School of Business (ISB — Hyderabad). Professor Capon currently holds the position of Distinguished Visiting Professor at Manchester Business School.

Professor Capon has published more than 60 journal articles and edited book chapters. Journals that have published his work include *Academy of Management Research*; *Academy of Management Review*; *American Journal of Public Health*; *Annals of Operations Research*; *California Management Review*; *Cognition and Instruction*; *Columbia Journal of World Business*; *Communication Research*; *Congressional Record*; *Developmental Psychology*; *Harvard Business Review*; *Industrial Marketing Management*; *Journal of Advertising Research*; *Journal of Applied Developmental Psychology*; *Journal of Applied Psychology*; *Journal of Business Administration*; *Journal of Consumer Research*; *Journal of Financial Services Research*; *Journal of International Business Studies*; *Journal of International Forecasting*; *Journal of Management Studies*; *Journal of Marketing*; *Journal of Marketing Research*; *Journal of Strategic Marketing*; *Laboratory of Comparative Human Cognition*; *Management Decision*; *Management Science*; *Public Opinion Quarterly*; *Review of Marketing*; *Strategic Management Journal*; and *Transactions of the Faraday Society*. Professor Capon has published more than 20 books, including: *Corporate Strategic Planning*, a major study of the planning practices of major U.S. manufacturing corporations (Columbia University Press 1988); *The Marketing of Financial Services: A Book of Cases* (Prentice-Hall 1992); *Planning the Development of Builders, Leaders and Managers of Twenty First Century Business* (Kluwer Academic Publishers 1996) on the curriculum review process at Columbia Business School; *Why Some Firms Perform Better than Others: Towards a More Integrative Explanation* (Kluwer Academic Publishers 1996) on the underpinnings of superior corporate financial performance; *The Asian Marketing Case Book* (Prentice Hall 1999); *Marketing Management in the 21st Century* (Prentice Hall 2001); *Key Account Management and Planning* (Free Press 2001); and *Total Integrated Marketing* (Free Press, 2003).

More recently, Professor Capon has published *The Marketing Mavens* (Crown Business 2007) and *Managing Global Accounts* (Wessex, 2008); two new textbooks, *Managing Marketing in the 21st Century* (U.S. edition, Wessex 2007; European edition, Wessex 2008) and *Capon's Marketing Framework* (Wessex 2009); a companion marketing planning workbook, *The Virgin Marketer* (Wessex 2007); and several Student Study Guides. Professor Capon's textbooks are also published in Chinese, Russian, and Spanish. In an attempt to reduce the high cost of college textbooks, students can secure Wessex's textbooks as traditional print versions and pdf e-books, or access them FREE online for 14 days at *www.axcesscapon.com*, then *pay what they think it's worth*!

In addition to teaching in Columbia Business School's MBA and Executive MBA programs, Professor Capon is active in executive education. He has directed *Competitive Marketing Strategy*, *Strategic Account Management*, *Sales Management*, and *Strategic Pricing* programs. In addition, he has directed and taught executive seminars for leading business schools and corporations around the world. Professor Capon inaugurated Columbia Business School's highly successful executive-level *Marketing Management* program as a joint venture in Shanghai, PRC with CEIBS and the Global Account Manager Certification program with St. Gallen University in Switzerland.

PREFACE

The author developed *Strategic Account Strategy* over many years of working with organizations large and small on their account management programs — key, strategic, and global. In countless executive programs and workshops, he has helped executives struggle with developing strategic account programs and individual strategic account plans. In turn, participating executives have helped the author refine his own ideas on managing strategic accounts.

This volume comprises a set of frameworks in two books. Book 1, *The Strategic Account Program*, focuses on developing strategy for the strategic account program as a whole; Book 2, *Planning for Strategic Accounts*, is designed to assist strategic account managers prepare their strategic account plans. The frameworks in Book 1 and Book 2 are equally useful for programs and accounts that are domestic, regional, or global in scope. Book 1 will be useful for firms that are in the process of developing or reassessing their strategic account programs; we expect the major users of Book 2 to be account managers developing their own strategic account plans. Just as we believe that Book 1 is useful for account managers seeking to understand the internal environment of the strategic account program within which they manage their strategic accounts, we also believe the strategic account planning framework has considerable value at the strategic account program level. A common planning approach enhances roll-ups across strategic accounts and enables account-to-account comparisons.

In the account management field there is some terminological confusion — we hear *key*, *strategic*, *global*, *global-key*, and other *account* modifiers. All of these terms are designed to separate one special group of important customers from the rest. For the remainder of the book, we use the term *strategic* to encapsulate these terms. All we mean by *strategic account* is that to *lose* or *gain* such a customer would be a big deal for the firm.

Book 1 comprises four chapters: strategy for the strategic account program (Chapter 1), nominating and selecting strategic accounts (Chapters 2 and 3), and exploring various strategic issues for the strategic account program (Chapter 4).

Book 2 comprises four parts and eight chapters, two chapters per part. Part 1 — the strategic account strategy — focuses on the content and process for developing the strategic account plan. We lay out the content of the strategic account strategy and action programs so the strategic account manager is clear about the purpose of the plan (Chapter 1). We then provide a suggested process for completing the plan (Chapter 2). Part 2 contains the meat of the matter for strategic account managers — the situation analysis: strategic account insight (Chapter 3) and competitor and firm insight (Chapter 4). Part 3 — bridge to strategy — follows logically from the situation analysis: planning assumptions (Chapter 5) and opportunities and threats (Chapter 6). Finally, Part 4 develops strategy and implementation: the strategic account strategy (Chapter 7) and action at the strategic account (Chapter 8).

This is not a large volume. Readers do most of the work when they complete the frameworks and develop strategy for the strategic account program — Book 1, or strategic account plans for individual strategic accounts — Book 2. We hope that the frameworks in this book will help you to approach your strategic customers more strategically, at both the strategic account program and individual strategic account levels, and bring enhanced value both to your strategic customers and your firm.

Contact Professor Capon (*nc7@columbia.edu*) for a full set of electronic templates.

TABLE OF CONTENTS

THE STRATEGIC
ACCOUNT PROGRAM

THIS BOOK COMPRISES FOUR CHAPTERS. In Chapter 1, we lay out the strategy for the strategic account program. In Chapter 2, we nominate strategic accounts. In Chapter 3, we select strategic accounts from those that satisfied the nomination criteria. Finally, in Chapter 4, we explore various strategic issues for the strategic account program.

Chapter 1

Strategy for the
Strategic Account Program

THE PURPOSE OF THIS CHAPTER IS TO LAY OUT THE CORE ELEMENTS OF THE STRATEGIC ACCOUNT PROGRAM. Program definition is critical for the firm and for the strategic account manager. For the firm, the strategic account program strategy specifies its approach to major current and potential customers. For strategic account managers, the strategy describes the internal environment in which they operate. By understanding strategy for the account program, strategic account managers do a better job of strategy and action program development for their own strategic accounts. Hence, we believe that both senior managers and strategic account managers should identify the current program strategy but also to suggest modifications.

PROGRAM DEFINITION

We commence by laying out the parameters of the strategic account program. Specifically, we want to capture both the Business/Product Definition and the Geographic Definition. Of course, some strategic account programs function at the corporate level; others are based in business units.

Figure 1.1: Strategic Account Program Definition

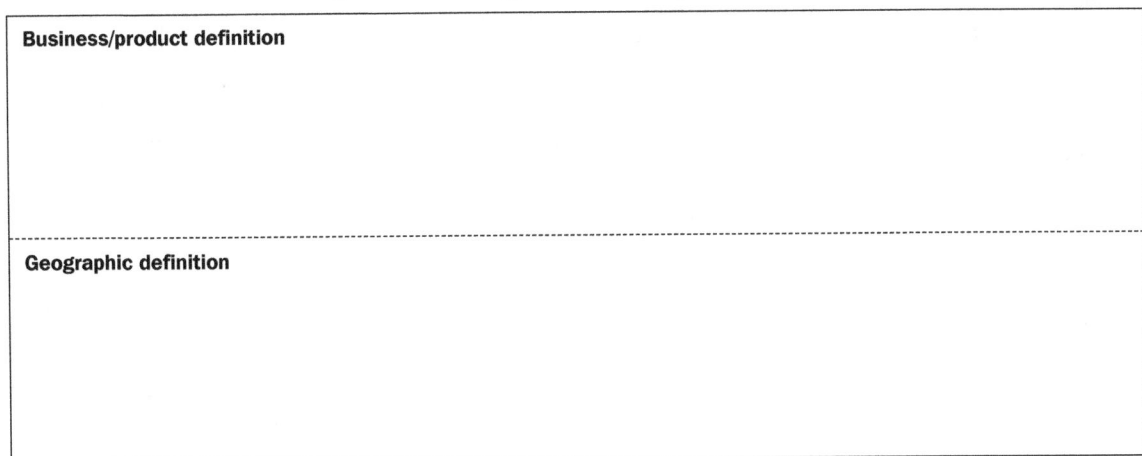

Business/product definition

Geographic definition

VISION

Vision provides focus and direction for the strategic account program and should be stated as a *journey* rather than as a *destination*. Examples of vision statements are:

- **Milliken Carpet Organization:** To develop strategic alliances with our global corporate customers by organizing teams focused on providing total customer satisfaction at the lowest possible process cost

- **Cisco:** To provide best-in-class business practices and support to our worldwide strategic account customers

Figure 1.2: Vision for the Strategic Account Program

Our strategic account program's vision statement:

Proposal for our strategic account program's vision statement:

BRANDING

Branding is an important element in most firm's marketing efforts. The firm aims most branding activities at external constituencies, mainly customers, to reduce uncertainly and change attitudes and behavior. Branding is also important within the organization to change attitudes and behavior of organizational members. Branding the strategic account program can help communicate the vision and secure organizational buy-in and support.

Figure 1.3: Branding the Strategic Account Program

	Currently	Should Be
• **Name of my account management program**		
• **Logo**		
• **Communication strategy:**		
• **Communications objectives**		
• **Communications targets**		
• **Communications tools**		

PROGRAM SCOPE

Some strategic account programs are large, involving many customers and accounting for a large percentage of firm/business unit revenues; others are much more modest. We ask you to identify the current program scope and the planned steady state.

Figure 1.4: Strategic Account Program Scope

	Currently	Planned Steady State
• Number of strategic accounts		
• Strategic account revenues as a percentage of firm/business revenues		
• How the firm will move from *currently* to *planned steady state*		

ORGANIZATIONAL COMMITMENT

A critical element in the success of a strategic account program is the degree of organizational commitment. Commitment comes in several forms including overt support from top management, program funding, and the organizations approach to strategic account managers.

Figure 1.5: Organizational Commitment to the Strategic Account Program

	Currently	Should Be
• Overt support from top management		
• Program funding		

• Strategic account managers:
  • Compensation
 	
  • Expenses
 	
  • Technical support
 	
  • Empowerment		

TYPE OF CUSTOMER RELATIONSHIP

The firm may have several different types of relationship with its strategic accounts, ranging from partnership, through quality supplier, to vendor. Generally, suppliers like partnership relationships, but these tend to be expensive to develop and maintain. For an individual strategic account, different business areas may have different types of relationship. We ask you to estimate the percentage of revenues in each of these categories across the entire strategic account program — currently and what they should be — and suggest actions to close any gaps.

Figure 1.6: Type of Customer Relationship (percent) in the Strategic Account Program

	Currently	Should Be
• Partner		
• Quality supplier		
• Vendor		
Proposed actions to reduce the gaps:		

NOMINATING AND SELECTING STRATEGIC ACCOUNTS

THE FIRM SHOULD ENTER CUSTOMERS INTO THE STRATEGIC ACCOUNT PROGRAM CAREFULLY. Bad choices are costly: a customer that should not be in the program consumes valuable resources and, moreover, excludes a customer that should be in the program. A good process for entering customers into the strategic account program includes both a nomination phase and a selection phase. A rigorous nomination and selection process is important for heading off internal political pressure from senior executives to put favored customers into the strategic account program.

Chapter 2

Nominating Strategic Accounts

THE PURPOSE OF A NOMINATION PROCESS IS TO IDENTIFY A SET OF POTENTIAL STRATEGIC ACCOUNTS. The sorts of criteria firms employ include current and potential revenues, geographic scope, and technological sophistication. The process may include both top-down and bottom-up nomination. Successfully nominated customers then move on to a selection phase.

Figure 2.1: Nominating Customers for the Strategic Account Program

	Currently	Should Be
My firm's criteria for nominating customers to be strategic accounts are:		
My firm's process for nominating customers to be strategic accounts is:		

Chapter 3
Selecting Strategic Accounts

THE SELECTION PROCESS IS TYPICALLY MORE INVOLVED THAN THE NOMINATION PROCESS and requires deeper analysis of individual candidate strategic accounts. Figure 3.1 illustrates the completion of the selection analysis. With this chart in hand the firm makes selection decisions. Key features of Figure 3.1 are:

- **Y-axis.** Measures the attractiveness of candidate strategic accounts to the firm.

- **X-axis.** Measures the ability of the firm to be successful at the strategic account.

- **Position of chart entries.** Assesses each candidate strategic account on attractiveness and business strengths.

- **Form of chart entries.** Size of filled-in circle measures current revenues (or other metric); open circle measures potential revenues (or other metric).

The completed chart does not tell the firm which candidate strategic accounts to accept. Actual selection depends on many other factors like the current portfolio of strategic accounts and resource availability.

Figure 3.1: Illustration of Selecting Strategic Accounts: Where We're Headed

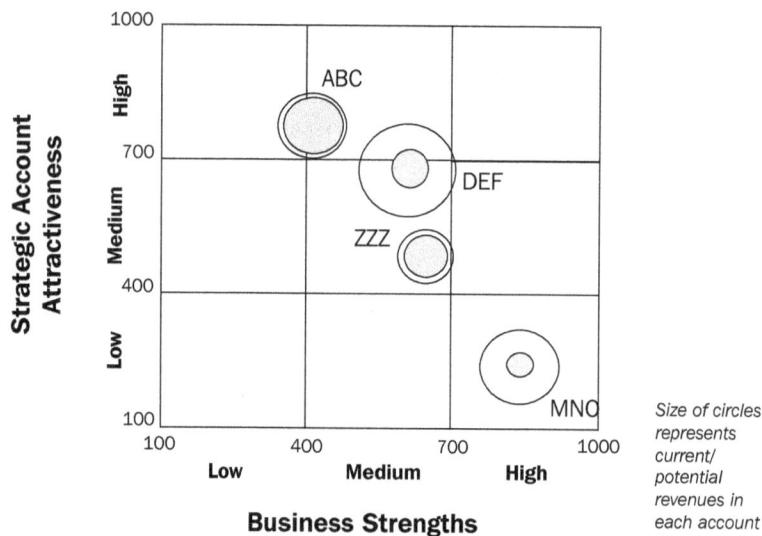

The data that generated the sizes of the circles in Figure 3.1 are in Figure 3.2.

Figure 3.2: Illustration of the Firm's Current and Potential Revenues

	Current Revenues	Potential Revenues
Strategic account ABC	95	100
Strategic account DEF	50	180
Strategic account MNO	30	120
Strategic account ZZZ	85	90
Etc.		

STRATEGIC ACCOUNT ATTRACTIVENESS

Step 1A: Brainstorm attractiveness factors. The first step in measuring the attractiveness of candidate strategic accounts is to brainstorm those factors that make strategic accounts attractive to the firm. "Our firm likes strategic accounts whose …" A useful categorization of factors is direct revenues and profits, organizational interrelationships (coherence with firm strategy, cultural fit), and potential revenues and profits. Examples include:

- Revenue is growing

- Revenue is continuous (versus periodic or episodic)

- Future revenues are assured

- Profit margins are high

- Culture fits ours well

- Top managers are opinion leaders in the industry

Figure 3.3: Brainstorm Attractiveness Criteria

"Our firm likes strategic accounts whose … "

Step 1B: Consolidate attractiveness factors. Select six to eight attractiveness factors (combining items if necessary) from **Step 1A** and enter in the left column of Figure 3.5.

Steps 2 through 5 require completion of a chart similar to the illustration in Figure 3.4. Use the chart in Figure 3.5.

Figure 3.4: Illustration of Attractiveness for Candidate Strategic Accounts

Criteria of Attractiveness	Weight	Candidate Strategic Accounts							
"Our firm likes strategic accounts whose ..."	(1–100)	ABC		DEF		MNO		ZZZ	
		Rating (1–10)	Score	Rating (1–10)	Score	Rating (1–10)	Score	Rating (1–10)	Score
Revenue is growing	15	5	75	4	60	1	15	6	90
Revenue is continuous	35	10	350	9	315	3	105	5	175
Future revenues are assured	15	10	150	7	105	1	15	7	105
Profit margins are high	10	3	30	3	30	4	40	3	30
Culture fits ours well	10	10	100	5	50	1	10	6	60
Top managers are opinion leaders in the industry	15	6	90	8	120	4	60	2	30
Totals:	**100**		**795**		**680**		**245**		**490**

Figure 3.5: Attractiveness for Candidate Strategic Accounts

Criteria of Attractiveness	Weight	Candidate Strategic Accounts							
"Our firm likes strategic accounts whose ..."	(1–100)	1. Name:		2. Name:		3. Name:		4. Name:	
		Rating (1–10)	Score	Rating (1–10)	Score	Rating (1–10)	Score	Rating (1–10)	Score
Totals:	**100**								

Step 2: Attractiveness quotient. Assign weights to each criterion that reflects its importance to your firm. The weights must sum to 100.

Step 3: Candidate strategic account rating. Rate each candidate strategic account for each criterion identified in Step 1B. Use a 1-to-10 scale (1 = strong disagreement, 10 = strong agreement), and set minimum cut-off ratings such that a candidate strategic account would be excluded if its rating were insufficiently high on an individual criterion. *Hint:* When rating several candidate strategic accounts, it is easier to proceed by rating all accounts criterion-by-criterion, rather than rating each account on all criteria.

Step 4: Attractiveness factor. Multiply the Attractiveness Quotient times the Strategic Account Rating for each criterion.

Step 5: Candidate strategic account attractiveness total score. Add all the answers to calculate a total. *Note:* Totals range from 100 for most unattractive to 1000 for most attractive.

BUSINESS STRENGTHS

The firm must conduct the business strengths analysis for each candidate strategic account separately.

Step 1A: Brainstorm business strength factors. For each candidate strategic account, the firm must brainstorm answers to the question: "To succeed at this strategic account, any supplier must possess...," using Figure 3.6. Examples include:

- Low cost operations

- Established distribution facilities

- Strong sales force

- Effective information systems

- Ability to innovate new products

- Deep pockets

Figure 3.6: Brainstorm Business Strengths Criteria

"To succeed at this strategic account, any supplier must possess ..."	
Candidate Strategic Account 1	**Candidate Strategic Account 2**

"To succeed at this strategic account, any supplier must possess ..."	
Candidate Strategic Account 3	**Candidate Strategic Account 4**

Step 1B: Consolidate business strength factors. For each candidate strategic account, select six to eight business strengths (combining items if necessary) from **Step 1A** and enter in the left column of Figure 3.8.

Steps 2 through 5 require completion of charts similar to the illustration in Figure 3.7. Use the charts in Figure 3.8.

Step 2: Business strengths quotient. Assign weights to each business strength that reflects its importance in succeeding at the candidate strategic account. The weights must sum to 100.

Step 3: Rate your firm. Rate your firm on its possession of each of the business strengths identified in Step 1B with respect to the candidate strategic account. Use a 1-to-10 scale (1 = very weak, 10 = very strong).

Step 4: Business strengths factor. Multiply the Business Strengths Quotient times Your Firm's Rating for each business strength.

Step 5: Business strengths total score. Add all the answers to calculate a total. Totals range from 100 for least business strength to 1000 for most business strength.

Figure 3.7: Illustration of Business Strengths Analysis

Business Strengths	Strategic Account ABC			Business Strengths	Strategic Account DEF		
"To succeed at Candidate Strategic Account ABC, any supplier must possess..."	**Weighting (1–100)**	**Firm Rating (1–10)**	**Score**	*"To succeed at Candidate Strategic Account DEF, any supplier must possess..."*	**Weighting (1–100)**	**Firm Rating (1–10)**	**Score**
Good R&D	15	3	45	Low cost operations	20	5	100
Established distribution facilities	20	4	80	Established distribution facilities	10	9	90
Strong sales force	25	5	125	Strong sales force	10	7	70
Good technical service organization	20	2	40	Effective information systems	20	6	120
Ability to innovate new products/services	10	6	60	Ability to innovate new products	15	10	150
Fast-moving organization	10	7	70	Deep pockets	25	3	75
Totals:	**100**		**420**	*Totals:*	**100**		**605**

Figure 3.8: Business Strengths Analysis

Business Strengths *"To succeed at this Candidate Strategic Account, any supplier must possess…"*	1. Name:		
	Weighting (1–100)	**Firm Rating (1–10)**	**Score**
Totals:	**100**		

Business Strengths *"To succeed at this Candidate Strategic Account, any supplier must possess…"*	2. Name:		
	Weighting (1–100)	**Firm Rating (1–10)**	**Score**
Totals:	**100**		

Business Strengths *"To succeed at this Candidate Strategic Account, any supplier must possess…"*	3. Name:		
	Weighting (1–100)	**Firm Rating (1–10)**	**Score**
Totals:	**100**		

Business Strengths *"To succeed at this Candidate Strategic Account, any supplier must possess…"*	4. Name:		
	Weighting (1–100)	**Firm Rating (1–10)**	**Score**
Totals:	**100**		

STRATEGIC ACCOUNT ATTRACTIVENESS/BUSINESS STRENGTHS CHART

To develop the chart for displaying the results of the analysis (Figure 3.11), we develop two additional figures. In Figure 3.9, you summarize the results of the strategic account attractiveness and business strengths analyses. In Figure 3.10, you assess current and potential revenues for each candidate strategic account.

Figure 3.9: Summary of Strategic Account Attractiveness and Business Strengths Analyses

Strategic Account	Strategic Account Attractiveness Score	Business Strengths Score
1.		
2.		
3.		
4.		

Figure 3.10: The Firm's Current and Potential Revenues by Strategic Account

	Current Revenues	Potential Revenues
Strategic account 1		
Strategic account 2		
Strategic account 3		
Strategic account 4		
Etc.		

Using the data in Figure 3.9 and 3.10, plot the candidate strategic accounts in Figure 3.11.

Figure 3.11: Strategic Account Attractiveness/Business Strengths Analysis

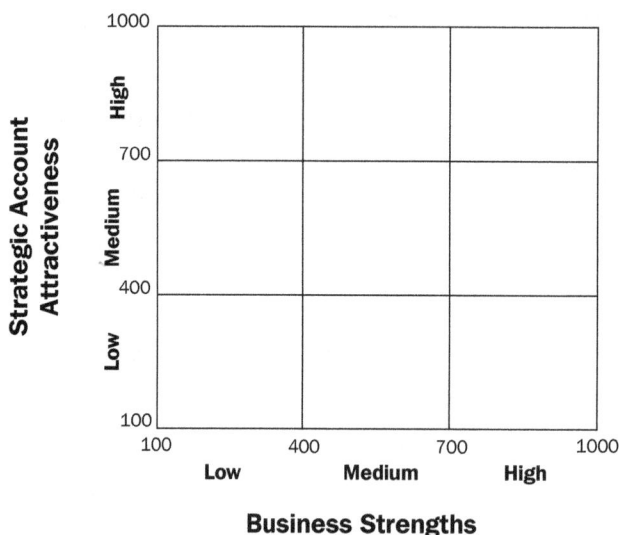

Business Strengths

Figure 3.12 provides you with the opportunity to reflect on your firm's strategic account selection process and to make recommendations for improvements.

Figure 3.12: Review the Strategic Account Selection Process

My firm's process for selecting strategic accounts is:

Recommendations for improving the strategic account selection process:

CHAPTER 4

Strategic Issues for the Strategic Account Program

PORTFOLIO COMPOSITION

In this section, we address several issues concerning composition of your firm's strategic account portfolio. Enter your responses in Figure 4.1

Tiering. Many firms do not construct just a single strategic account portfolio, but rather recognize that customers can be strategic accounts at several different levels or tiers.

Portfolio evaluation. The firm's portfolio of strategic accounts, or individual portfolio tiers, is not static, but evolves over time; current strategic accounts become less attractive and non-strategic accounts become candidates for inclusion in the strategic account program. Making these decisions requires an evaluation process for current strategic accounts.

Disengagement. As the portfolio evolves, it may be necessary to drop a strategic account down from a higher to a lower tier or even move them out of the program altogether.

Figure 4.1: Issues in Strategic Account Portfolio Composition

	Currently	Should Be
Tiering **My firm's approach to tiering:**		
Continuous evaluation **My firm's approach to continuous evaluation:**		
Disengagement **My firm's approach to disengagement:**		

STRATEGY FOR STRATEGIC ACCOUNTS

The process of working through strategy for the strategic account program, and nominating and selecting strategic accounts, may have given you ideas for improving your firm's strategic account strategy. Figure 4.2 provides you with the opportunity to suggest options.

Figure 4.2: Improving the Firm's Strategic Account Strategy

Major actions the firm should take (ease/difficulty of making changes):
1.
2.
3.
4.
5.
6.

BOOK 2

PLANNING FOR
STRATEGIC ACCOUNTS

PART 1

THE STRATEGIC ACCOUNT STRATEGY

CHAPTER 1

Elements of the Strategic Account Strategy

THE STRATEGIC ACCOUNT STRATEGY LAYS OUT IN VERY CLEAR TERMS actions that the firm plans to take regarding the strategic account. Specific actions sit within a broad strategy framework of how the strategic account manager intends to address the strategic account — Figure 1.1. We partition elements of the strategy into three broad areas — approaching the strategic account, direction of effort, and action programs.

APPROACHING THE STRATEGIC ACCOUNT

The strategic account approach comprises three core elements — vision, mission, and performance objectives.

VISION

The vision states in broad terms how the firm plans to treat the strategic account and provides focus and direction for the strategic account manager. The vision statement is not a goal; it should be stated as a *journey* rather than as a *destination*. In addition to a customer focus, the vision statement should also contain a firm focus. Generally, a strategic account's vision statement evolves slowly.

Vision statement illustrations are:

- Our vision for Huddersfield Inc. is to develop and grow a strategic alliance so we provide total customer satisfaction at the lowest possible process cost. Executing our vision will enhance our position at Huddersfield and improve our financial returns.

- We shall be recognized as Wigan's preferred supplier of innovative environmental resource services and hence gain the lion's share of its business.

- We shall continually push the envelope to provide best-in-class business practice and support to Doncaster, Inc. and solidify our position as its preferred supplier.

Figure 1.1: Schematic of the Strategic Account Strategy

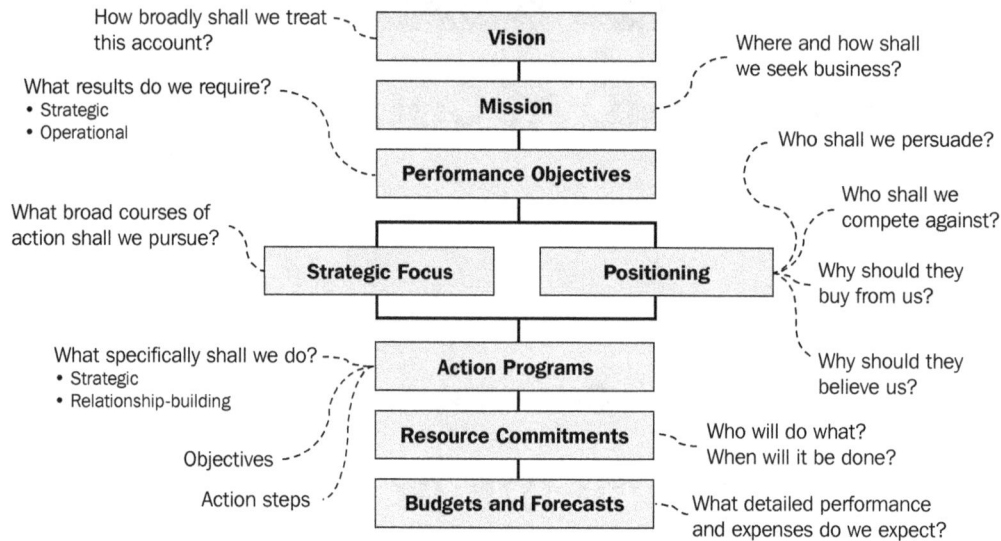

MISSION

Whereas *vision* states the firm's general approach to the strategic account, *mission* identifies specific areas of the account from which the firm intends to secure revenues. Many firms' strategic accounts comprise customers that operate multiple business units, with multiple departments, in multiple geographic areas. Rarely does the firm secure revenues from the entire strategic account. Typically, certain business units, departments, and/or geographies represent the most attractive opportunities. The purpose of the mission is to identify those areas where the strategic account manager plans to search for opportunities.

Mission statement illustrations are:

- We shall deploy our new Super Max technology to maintain historic revenue share in Huddersfield's North American and European operations. But we shall place renewed emphasis on securing increased growth and higher share in Huddersfield's Asia Pacific region with our traditional products.

- We shall focus efforts at Wigan on our new Matverse products in the U.S. and Latin America. Correspondingly, we shall continue to put major effort on current products in Wigan's Europe and Asia Pacific regions.

PERFORMANCE OBJECTIVES

Performance objectives specify results that the firm intends to achieve at the strategic account — they contain both strategic and operational elements.

- **Strategic objectives** — qualitative and directional, typically stated in terms of growth, market share, or profits.

    Illustration: Our strategic objective at Huddersfield is to increase revenues.

    Illustration: Our strategic objective at Wigan is to maintain revenues while increasing margins.

- **Operational objectives** — quantitative and time dependent. The firm states operational objectives both for the short term — typically one year, and the long term — typically three years. These anticipated results help the firm determine the appropriate resource commitments to the account. The statement of operational objectives includes the strategic objective.

Example: Our objective at Huddersfield is to increase revenues during the next three years:

  - In 20XY (next year), revenues will increase 30 percent from $15 million to $19.5 million.

  - In 20XY+2, revenues will reach $25 million.

DIRECTION OF EFFORT

The broad approach to applying effort at the strategic account encompasses two major elements — strategic focus and positioning.

STRATEGIC FOCUS

The strategic focus specifies in general terms the broad courses of action the firm will pursue to achieve its performance objectives at the strategic account. We take as our starting point a performance objective of improving the firm's return on investment (ROI). Essentially, as Figure 1.2 shows, the firm has two broad ways of achieving this objective — increase sales units or improve margins and investment returns.

In general, if the firm's strategic performance objectives are *growth and market share*, major efforts should focus on *increasing sales units*. Conversely, if the firm's performance objectives focus on *enhancing cash flow* from the account, it would most likely focus efforts on *improving margins and investment returns*. A performance objective of *increased profits* would balance efforts on the two branches.

Figure 1.2: Strategic Focus

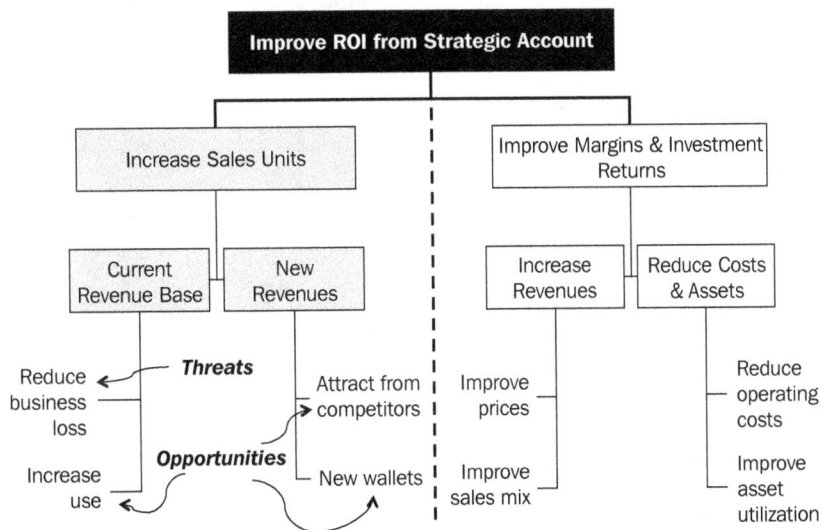

- **Increase sales units.** The firm can increase sales units by securing more sales from the *current revenue base*, or gain *new revenues*.

- **Current revenue base.** The firm is under constant threat from competitors trying to steal its business — it does a better job of repelling these *threats* by *reducing business lost*. Or the strategic account's *increases use* of the firm's current products.
- **New revenues.** The firm secures new revenues by *attracting from competitors*, or opens up *new wallets* — persuading the strategic account to purchase the firm's products for new applications.

- **Improve margins and investment returns.** The firm can improve margins and investment returns by either *increasing revenues* or *reducing costs and assets*, holding sales units constant.
    - **Increase revenues.** The firm increases revenues either by *increasing prices* or by *improving the sales mix* — selling more high margin items or fewer low margin items.
    - **Reduce costs and assets.** The firm can reduce *operating costs* or *improve asset utilization* — like reducing dedicated fixed investment or accounts receivable.

POSITIONING

The positioning statement, illustrated in Figure 1.3, has four core elements:

- **Customer target.** The strategic account manager should specify the various decision-makers, influencers, information providers, and other individuals who are important for securing the firm's performance objectives at the strategic account.

- **Competitor target.** Competitor targets are those firms that seek the same revenue wallets as the firm. The strategic account manager should be very clear about what organizations and individuals the firm is up against.

- **Value proposition.** The value proposition states broadly why the strategic account should do business with the firm rather than with its competitive targets. Of course, different individuals within the strategic account will have different reasons. The job of the strategic account manager is to capture these requirements in a single value proposition.

- **Reason to believe.** Promising value is one thing; delivering that value is quite another. The strategic account manager must be able to demonstrate to the firm's customer targets that the firm can indeed deliver on its promises.

Figure 1.3: Cemex Positioning for Multinational Contracting Firm

Task	Focus	Positioning Item
Convince	Multinational contracting firm's corporate leaders and geographic heads	**Customer target**
In the context of other alternatives	Traditional cement producers	**Competitor target**
That they will receive these benefits	Consistent delivery within 30 minutes of Cemex receiving an order (versus the 3-hour standard)	**Value proposition**
Because we have these capabilities	A global positioning satellite system on each truck, and computer software that combines truck positions with plant output and customer orders to calculate optimal destinations and make en route redirections.	**Reason to believe**

We should be very clear that this positioning statement concerns the overall relationship between the firm and strategic account. For separate opportunities, different individuals may be involved in the decision, the firm may be up against different competitors, and value propositions and reasons to believe may be very specific.

ACTION AT THE STRATEGIC ACCOUNT

Two areas are important — action programs and the resources for implementing them.

ACTION PROGRAMS

Action programs follow logically from the *direction of effort*. They specify the firm's future actions at the strategic account. Action programs come in two types — *strategic* action programs and *relationship-building* action programs. In each case, action programs should specify an objective and a series of action steps.

- **Strategic action programs.** Strategic action programs specify the actions the firm will take to secure revenues from the strategic account. These plans come in various shapes and sizes. We identify three broad types:
    - **Finding the opportunity.** The focus of this action program is a search for opportunity at the strategic account.
    - **Winning the business.** The strategic account manager has identified an opportunity — the action program focuses on winning the business.
    - **Signed contract.** The strategic account manager has secured a signed contract — the action program focuses on delivering the promised value.

- **Relationship-building action programs.** *Organizations* do not make decisions; *people in organizations* make decisions! The strategic account manager should continually work to improve the web of relationships between the firm's executives and executives at the strategic account, including his/her own relationships. Relationship-building action programs are the vehicle for accomplishing this task.

RESOURCES

The strategic account manager and firm management agree on the financial, human, and other resources required to implement the firm's various action programs.

Chapter 2

Developing the
Strategic Account Plan

IN THIS CHAPTER, WE FOCUS ON TWO ELEMENTS FOR DEVELOPING THE STRATEGIC ACCOUNT PLAN — process and framework.

PROCESS

There are many ways to develop the strategic account plan. We offer one five-step approach that many firms have found useful.

Step 1: Collect materials. Collect background materials for developing the strategic account plan. Includes but is not limited to: the prior year's plan, sales and profit results, action program results from prior year, status of initiatives, notes from inter-firm meetings, general background information on the strategic account.

Step 2: Offsite meeting. A two-day offsite meeting commences the planning process. Ideally, attendees at the first half-day include the account team and, most importantly, key strategic account personnel. The morning is given over to the strategic account, whose representatives lay out their business assumptions, objectives, and strategy for the up-coming year (and longer-term) and their assessment of implications for the supplier firm. After strategic account personnel leave, the account team prepares a rough draft of the account plan, highlighting questions that must be addressed in preparing the plan.

Step 3: Time period 6 to 8 weeks. The strategic account manager and team build on the offsite meeting to develop a tentative strategic account plan including strategy and action programs. Team members secure tentative buy-in internally for required resources to implement the plan.

Step 4: Half/1-day meeting. The strategic account manager and team present their proposed strategy and action programs to representatives from the strategic account. The purpose of this meeting is to secure definitive agreement to the firm's proposals from the strategic account.

Step 5: Time period 2 to 4 weeks. The strategic account manager and team finalize the strategy and action programs. They secure buy-in from relevant internal constituencies for the necessary resources to implement the strategy and action programs. This process included defining roles, securing the right people, agreeing key performance indicators (KPIs), and fixing schedules. The strategic account strategy and action programs are the basis for a high-level briefing document.

Figure 2.1: Illustration of the Planning Process

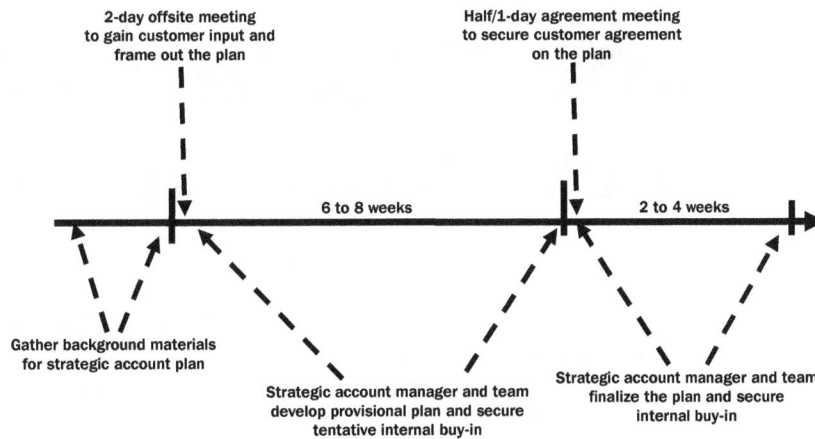

FRAMEWORK

Figure 2.2 shows a framework for developing the strategic account plan. The remainder of this book discusses each element in turn: Part 2 — Situation Analysis, Chapters 3 and 4; Part 3 — Bridge to Strategy, Chapters 5 and 6; and Part 4 — Strategy and Implementation, Chapters 7 and 8. Note that for customers with diversified business units, the strategic account manager may have to complete some elements of plan development multiple times.

Figure 2.2: Framework for Developing the Strategic Account Plan

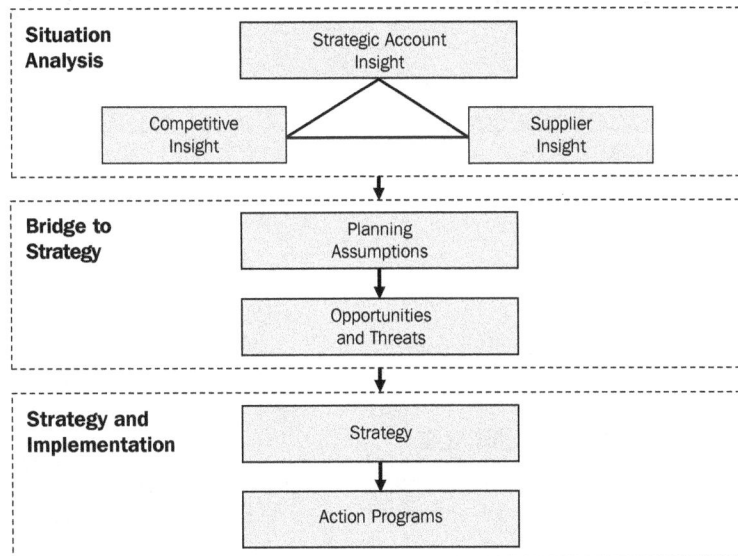

PART 2

SITUATION ANALYSIS

THE PURPOSE OF THE SITUATION ANALYSIS IS TO DEVELOP INSIGHT INTO YOUR STRATEGIC ACCOUNT — Chapter 3, as well as insight into your competitors and your own firm — Chapter 4. These insights will lead to a clear and deep understanding of the account, its business(es), and the trends and forces that it faces. In turn, this insight will help you uncover opportunities and threats for your firm.

CHAPTER 3

Core Strategic Account Insight

This chapter contains instructions for completing templates that will help you develop insight into your strategic account. Strategic account Insight comprises four analyses:

- Strategic Account Fundamentals
- Strategic Account Analysis
- Customer Value Analysis
- Purchase Process Analysis

STRATEGIC ACCOUNT FUNDAMENTALS

This analysis develops background information that you require for the strategic account analysis portion of the situation analysis. In turn, the strategic account analysis is critically important for developing the strategic account strategy.

The template for *Strategic Account Fundamentals* is in Figure 3.1. Your goal in completing this template should be to secure sufficient understanding and insight into the strategic account and the challenges it faces such that you could have an intelligent one-hour conversation with the strategic account's CEO. The topics listed are neither exclusive nor comprehensive; you should feel free to include additional dimensions for insight.

- **Ownership**
  - Identify the parent company, subsidiaries, ownership interests, partnerships
  - Who are the directors, principal owners? Are they active or passive?
  - Where are corporate offices located?
  - Public company or private? Where are its shares listed?

- **Organization**
  - Centralized or decentralized?
  - Global organization? If so, does it have a domestic U.S. division and a separate international division, geographic area divisions, strategic product divisions, or some other kind of structure?
  - How are developments in telecommunications, computer technology, and the Internet affecting the strategic account's organization structure and processes?

- **Top management**
  - Who are the CEO and other members of top management? Are they succeeding at their goals? Do they have the confidence of the board of directors or is there a difficult relationship?
  - What are their business and management philosophies?
  - What is the corporate culture? What is current capacity utilization?
  - What vision and values (if any) have they articulated?

- **Locations**
  - Where are the fixed assets located?
  - Where are the plants?
  - What are the plants' capacities?
  - How many employees does each location have? How are employees distributed across locations?

- **Corporate actions**
  - Major resource shifts, significant capital spending, mergers, acquisitions, divestitures, joint ventures, R&D initiatives, new product introductions, increased internationalization, new market entry, use of the Internet, participation in B2B exchanges....
  - How successful have these been?

- **Financial performance**
  - Revenue and profit history — overall and for relevant business units and geographies
  - Trends for return on assets, stock price, earnings per share
  - What's the debt/equity ratio? How is the account's debt rated?
  - What financial ratios are important?
  - How does performance compare to major competitors?

- **Future prospects**
  - What is the long-run outlook?
  - Does it face any significant legal/regulator problems?
  - How is it perceived by the financial community? Do the majority of financial analysts recommend sell, hold, or buy? Why?

- **Timing**
  - What are the time cycles — for example, the planning and budgeting cycle?
  - What are important dates — for example, the fiscal year and annual meetings?
  - Is there a periodicity to important announcements such as CEO meetings with financial analysts?

Figure 3.1: Strategic Account Fundamentals

Element	Your Analysis and Insight
Ownership	
Organization	
Top management	
Locations	
Corporate actions	
Financial performance	
Future prospects	
Timing	

STRATEGIC ACCOUNT ANALYSIS

This analysis develops a more detailed understanding of the strategic account. It includes an analysis of *external factors* that impact the strategic account's ability to secure revenues; an analysis of the strategic account's *internal processes*; and an analysis of *Strategic Coherence* — how realistic the account is about its goals and objectives.

The templates for *Strategic Account Analysis* are in Figure 3.2 to Figure 3.4.

External Analysis

For each of the following items, the strategic account manager should describe the situation, then identify implications for the strategic account.

- **Market**
  - What market(s) does the account sell into?
  - What products does it sell?
  - What services does it offer?

- **Environment**
  - What political pressures does the account face?
  - What legal or regulatory issues are there?
  - Are there social or demographic trends that impact the account's business?
  - What technological trends or changes are there?
  - Are there other factors that impact the account's ability to compete, but over which it has little or no control?

- **Competitive structure**
  - What types of competition does the account face?
  - Direct and indirect
  - Actual and potential
  - Where are new competitors coming from?
  - What forces are shaping the competitive structure?

- **Competitors**
  - What are the account's specific competitive threats?

- **Customers**
  - To whom does the account sell?
  - What sort of entities are they?

Figure 3.2: Strategic Account Analysis — External Analysis

Item	Description	Implications for the Strategic Account
Market		
Environment		
Competitive structure		
Competitors		
Customers		

Internal Analysis

For each of the following items, the strategic account manager should describe the situation, then identify implications for the strategic account.

- **Strategic account's strategic thrust**
  - Objectives
  - Strategy
  - Major action programs

- **Strategic account's competence**
  - Strengths and weaknesses
  - Past performance

Figure 3.3: Strategic Account Analysis — Internal Analysis

Item		Description	Implications for the Strategic Account
Strategic Thrust	Objectives		
	Strategy		
	Major action programs		
Competence	Strengths & weaknesses		
	Past performance		

Strategic Coherence

- **Potential success.** Do you believe the strategic account can implement its strategy and achieve its stated objectives?
  - If so, what must the strategic account do to succeed?
  - If not, why not? What action(s) could the strategic account take to turn the situation around?

- **Opportunities.** Can your firm help make the strategic account's strategy coherent?

Figure 3.4: Strategic Account Analysis — Strategic Coherence

Can the strategic account succeed?	
Why or why not?	
What can your firm do to help?	

CUSTOMER VALUE ANALYSIS

This purpose of this analysis is to determine the strategic account's true needs and how your firm may satisfy those needs. Further, it will help you identify ways to satisfy unstated needs — these will help you gain differential advantage. Customer value analysis comprises two elements — *customer value ideas* and *customer value actions*. The templates for customer value analysis are in Figures 3.5 and 3.6.

Customer Value Ideas

The purpose of this analysis is to catalog and identify ways that the firm may bring value to the strategic account. In particular:

- **Value ideas in process.** Identify ways to bring new value to the strategic account that are either already underway or that you are already planning to implement.

- **New value ideas.** Brainstorm a list of "out of the box" ideas that will be more difficult to implement but perhaps more valuable to the customer.

Figure 3.5: Customer Value Ideas

Value Ideas in Process	New Value Ideas

Customer Value Actions

The purpose of this analysis is to specify the value to the customer of a select number of value ideas and to understand what the firm would have to do to deliver this value:

- **Top few ideas.** Identify the top few ideas from Figure 3.5 and the value they would bring to the account.

- **Required actions for top ideas.** Determine the steps required to enact these value ideas. What must happen for the firm to successfully implement these ideas?

Figure 3.6: Customer Value Actions

Idea	Value to the Customer	How to Make it Work

PURCHASE PROCESS ANALYSIS

This analysis is designed to further your understanding of how your strategic account chooses its vendors, and how you may influence those decisions in your favor.

Purchase Process and Use Flow Chart

Figure 3.7 provides a generic process of value and the customer experience that may prove helpful in mapping out your strategic account's process. You may use the empty chart in Figure 3.8 to develop the process for your strategic account.

- **Step 1: Create flow chart.** Create a flow chart showing all the steps in the strategic account's purchase and use process, from the initial trigger that sets the process in motion until the account disposes of/recycles the product.
  - Use rectangles for activities that don't require decisions.
  - Use diamonds for decision forks, and show the different paths for "yes" and "no" decisions.

- **Step 2: Specify the steps.** Identify by name and/or role the specific person or people involved in each step in the process.

- **Step 3: Note time required.** Indicate the time required for each step.

- **Step 4: Assess process.** Assess the process for stability and interface points. Where can your firm help to speed the process, or make it easier and/or more efficient for strategic account personnel?

Figure 3.7: Value and the Strategic Account Experience

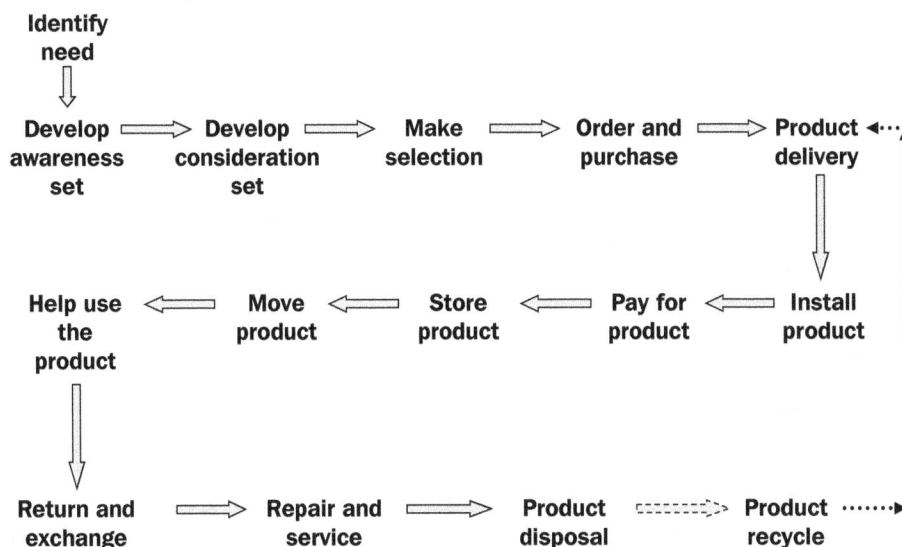

Identify
need
⇩

Develop ⟹ Develop ⟹ Make ⟹ Order and ⟹ Product ◄┈┐
awareness   consideration   selection   purchase   delivery   ┊
set   set   ┊
                                                                                    ⇓
Help use ⟸ Move ⟸ Store ⟸ Pay for ⟸ Install
the   product   product   product   product
product
⇩
Return and ⟹ Repair and ⟹ Product ┄┄┄┄⟫ Product ┈┈┈►
exchange   service   disposal   recycle

Figure 3.8: Value and the Strategic Account Experience

Identify
need
⇩

Decision Makers & Influencers

The purpose of this analysis is to identify key executives at the strategic account who, currently or potentially, have a role to play in the firm/strategic account relationship. For each key player identified in the Figure 3.8 process flow, identify the name, position, role, degree of influence, and other relevant information. Figure 3.9 provides a template for this analysis.

- **Identification.** Identify relevant strategic account executives by name.

- **Organizational position.** Specify the person's position in the strategic account organization.

- **Roles and degree of influence.** You should identify one or more persons for each of the following roles in the firm/strategic account relationship:

  - Decision-maker
  - Influencer (in the strategic account)
    - Spoiler
    - Champion

- Influencer (in third-party organizations)
- User
- Specifier
- Gatekeeper
- Information provider

- **Degree of influence.** Note each person's degree of influence within the strategic account organization.

- **Perception.** Assess each person's perception of your firm relative to competitors.

- **Relationships.** Assess each person's relationships with people in your firm relative to people in competitor firms.

- **Personal interests.** Determine each person's personal interests.

- **Reputation.** Determine each person's reputation within the strategic account and in the industry.

- **"Hot buttons."** Identify two or three "hot buttons" (motivational factors) for each person.

Figure 3.9: Decision Makers and Influencers

	Person 1	Person 2	Person 3
Organizational position			
Role in the firm/strategic account relationship			
Degree of influence			
Perceptions of your firm versus competitors			
Relationships with your firm versus competitors			
Personal interests			
Reputation within the strategic account and in the industry			
"Hot buttons"			

Note: Duplicate Figure 3.9 as many times as you need to cover all the key players at your strategic account.

CHAPTER 4

Competitor and Firm Insight

ONCE YOU HAVE FULLY ANALYZED YOUR STRATEGIC ACCOUNT — Chapter 3, the next step in the situation analysis is to understand those firms that compete with you for the strategic account's business. This chapter helps you to understand the competitive landscape, identify the most important competitors, determine their likely future courses of action, and understand the threat(s) they pose to your current and future business. A thorough analysis of competitors provides deep insight to your firm as a byproduct.

COMPETITIVE STRUCTURE ANALYSIS

Figure 4.1 shows a comprehensive view of competitive structure. For simplicity we separate out *indirect competitors*, and all others as forms of *direct competitors*.

Figure 4.1: The Structure of Competition

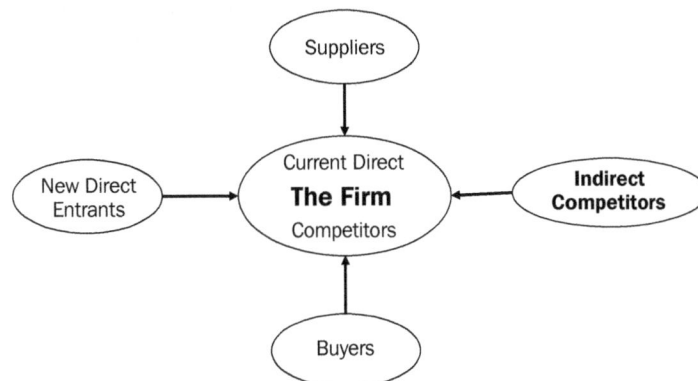

The templates for analyzing the competitive structure are in Figure 4.2:

- **Identify competitors.** Identify your direct and indirect competitors at the account, and sort them by whether they are actual or potential threats. Use the grid to help describe the competitive landscape.

- **Identify complementers.** Identify current and potential complementers (businesses that may help you at the account through mutual leverage).

- **Select.** Select three or four competitors that are of most concern to you.

Figure 4.2: Competitive Structure

| | Competitors | | Complementers |
	Direct	Indirect	
Actual			
Potential			

INDIVIDUAL COMPETITOR ANALYSIS

Templates for the individual competitor analysis are in Figure 4.3 and 4.5. Five steps are necessary to complete the competitive analysis. Two steps are general to all competitors; three steps are specific to each individual competitor. (This analysis is conceptually similar to the business strengths analysis in Book 1, Chapter 3.) The first two general steps are:

- **Step 1A: Brainstorm business strength factors.** Brainstorm answers to the question: "To succeed at this strategic account, *any* supplier must possess…" and enter in Figure 4.3.

- **Step 1B: Consolidate business strength factors.** Select six to eight business strengths (combining items if necessary from **Step 1A**) and enter in the left column of Figure 4.5. See Figure 4.4 for an illustration of this analysis.

- **Step 2: Business strengths quotient.** Assign weights to each business strength that reflects its importance in succeeding at the strategic account. The weights must sum to 100.

The next three steps are specific to each potential supplier to the strategic account; that is, your firm and the competitors you identified in Figure 4.2:

- **Step 3: Rate your firm and competitors.** Rate your firm and its competitors on possession of each of the business strengths identified in Step 1B. Use a 1-to-10 scale (1 = very weak, 10 = very strong).

- **Step 4: Business strengths factor.** Multiply the Business Strengths Quotient times the rating for your firm and each competitor on each business strength.

- **Step 5: Business strengths total score.** Add all the answers to calculate total scores for your firm and its competitors. Note: Totals range from 100 for least business strength to 1000 for most business strength.

The higher the business strengths score, the greater the probability of that supplier winning business at the strategic account. By comparing both the total scores and the scores for specific business strengths, you will secure a good idea of the relative strength of your firm versus competitors, and derive implications for your firm.

Figure 4.3: Brainstorm Business Strengths Criteria

"To succeed at this Strategic Account, any supplier must possess ..."

Figure 4.4: Illustration of Individual Competitor Analysis

Business Strengths *"To succeed in this strategic account, any supplier must possess..."*	Weight (1–100)	Your Firm		Competitor 1		Competitor 2		Competitor 3	
		Rating (1–10)	Score	Rating (1–10)	Score	Rating (1–10)	Score	Rating (1–10)	Score
Great products	20	6	120	5	100	7	140	5	100
Competent strategic account manager	15	5	75	4	60	3	45	8	120
Fast reponse customer service	10	7	70	6	60	4	40	3	30
Top-level engagement	10	6	60	5	50	2	20	7	70
Multiple distribution points	10	5	50	4	40	8	80	2	20
Just-in-time delivery system	15	4	60	5	75	7	105	2	30
Access to low-cost raw materials	10	5	50	6	60	2	20	2	20
Well-funded R&D	10	6	60	7	70	4	40	8	80
Totals	**100**		**645**		**515**		**490**		**470**

Figure 4.5: Individual Competitor Analysis

Business Strengths *"To succeed in this strategic account, any supplier must possess…"*	Weight (1–100)	Your Firm		Competitor 1		Competitor 2		Competitor 3	
		Rating (1–10)	Score	Rating (1–10)	Score	Rating (1–10)	Score	Rating (1–10)	Score
Totals	**100**								

Note: Duplicate the competitor columns in Figure 4.5 as many times as you need to cover all the major competitors at your strategic account.

COMPETITIVE PERFORMANCE AND STRATEGY ANALYSIS

This analysis builds on the individual competitor analysis — Figure 4.5. Its purpose is to assess the threats to your firm from competitive action at your strategic account. The template for this analysis is in Figure 4.6. The analysis comprises several steps:

- **Step 1: List competitors.** List the competitors in strength order according to your findings in the previous analysis and write down their total scores (from Figure 4.5).

- **Step 2: Detail position.** Detail each competitor's position (revenue share) at the strategic account. Use one of the following terms to describe competitive position:
    - Dominant
    - Tenable
    - Strong
    - Weak
    - Favorable

- **Step 3A: Assess current strategy/Step 3B: strengths and weaknesses.** Assess each competitor's strategy at the strategic account and summarize its strengths and weaknesses.

- **Step 4: Project competitor actions.** Based on the foregoing, what actions do you anticipate from competitors in the next one to three years? For example, will the competitor attempt to grow share or maximize profits? How?

- **Step 5: Threat analysis.** How serious a threat does each competitor's strategy pose to your firm?

- **Step 6: Options to thwart threats.** What options does your firm have to thwart these threats?

Figure 4.6: Competitor Performance and Strategy

		Competitor 1	Competitor 2	Competitor 3
About the Competitor	**Competitor (total score)**			
	Position (revenue share/ description)			
	Current strategy			
	Strengths and weaknesses			
	Project competitor actions			
About Your Firm	**Threat posed to your firm**			
	Options to combat threats			

Note: Duplicate the competitor columns in Figure 4.4 as needed to cover all major competitors at your strategic account.

PART 3

BRIDGE TO STRATEGY

ONCE YOU HAVE COMPLETED THE SITUATION ANALYSIS, the next step is to take the preparatory steps for developing your strategic account strategy and action programs. The core tasks are to develop assumptions about what the future might hold for your firm and your strategic account — Chapter 5, and to identify opportunities and threats for your firm and the strategic account — Chapter 6.

CHAPTER 5

Planning Assumptions

THE PLANNING ASSUMPTIONS EXERCISE IS A STRUCTURED TECHNIQUE for determining what events are likely to occur, and to what extent they are likely to impact your business at the strategic account. The templates for Planning Assumptions are in Figure 5.1 through Figure 5.3.

PLANNING ASSUMPTIONS LIST

The starting point for planning assumptions analysis is to identify many possible assumptions, their likelihood of occurrence, and their potential impact on the firm. We start with Figure 5.1:

- **List planning assumptions.** Brainstorm a list of events, trends, or business decisions that may impact your strategic account, your competitors, and/or your firm over the next one to three years. The list should include macro trends that affect all players, as well as micro events that would likely only impact a specific player. Number each planning assumption.

    - For each planning assumption, determine its likelihood of occurrence (low, medium, high) — relative to the other items.

    - For each planning assumption, determine how big an impact — positive or negative — it would have on your business at the strategic account (low, medium, high) — relative to all other items.

Figure 5.1: Planning Assumptions List

		Likelihood/Impact
About your strategic account		
About your competitors		
About your firm		
Other		

PLANNING ASSUMPTIONS MATRIX

The purpose of the Planning Assumptions Matrix is to separate out the various assumptions identified in the planning assumptions list. Figure 5.2 is helpful in this regard. Complete the following steps:

- **Step 1: Plot assumptions.** Plot each assumption (by number) you listed in Figure 5.1 based on its likelihood of occurrence and impact on the firm

- **Step 2: Assess impact on the firm.** Put a plus (+) or minus (–) on Figure 5.2 next to each planning assumption to show whether it would have a positive or negative impact on your firm if it occurred.

- **Step 3: Assess importance.** Identify the most important six to eight planning assumptions (those that fall above and to the right of the dashed line).

- **Step 4: Assess potential firm impact.** Indicate how much impact (high, medium, low) your firm could have on the assumption.

Figure 5.2: Planning Assumptions Matrix

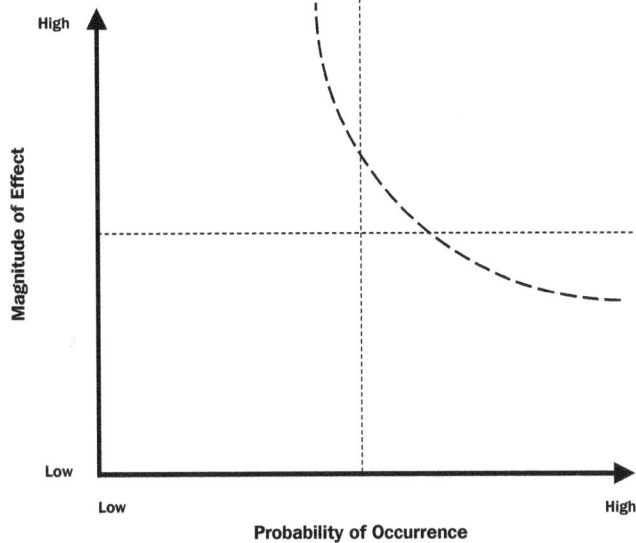

PLANNING ASSUMPTION STATEMENTS

The purpose of this exercise is to clarify your understanding of key assumptions regarding your strategic account. To start:

- **Step 1: Select assumptions.** Identify from Figure 5.2 the six or eight most important planning assumptions, based on likelihood of occurrence and impact on the firm (Step 3 in the previous exercise).

- **Step 2: "We believe."** Refine each original planning assumption item into a "we believe" statement for each of these most important planning assumptions.

- **Step 3: Implications.** Identify the implications for the firm of each of these most important planning assumptions

Figure 5.3: Planning Assumption Statements

"We Believe..."	Implications for Your Firm

CHAPTER 6

Opportunities and Threats

GIVEN WHAT YOU KNOW FROM THE SITUATION ANALYSIS — Chapters 3 and 4, and Planning Assumptions — Chapter 5, the next step is to determine the opportunities for new business and threats to your existing business. The relevant background and templates for identifying opportunities and threats are in Figure 6.1 through Figure 6.4.

OPPORTUNITIES

Broadly speaking, there are two avenues for improving business at your strategic account — you can *increase sales units* or *improve the margins and investment returns* of the business you're already doing. We have identified four methods for increasing sales units, and four methods for improving margins and investment returns. We summarize these eight methods in Figure 6.1. You may use these options to guide your search for opportunity at the strategic account.

Figure 6.1: Options for Increasing Sales Units and Margins and Investment Returns

	Increase sales units
Increase sales units	**Current revenue base** 1. **Reduce business lost.** Protect/maintain shares of current wallets 2. **Increase use.** Help strategic account to grow revenues (current business)
	New revenues 3. **Attract from competitors.** 4. **New wallets.** Help strategic account to grow revenues (new business)/ take over more value-added from strategic account (in-source)
	Improve margins and investment returns
Improve margins & investment returns	**Current revenue base** 5. **Improve prices.** 6. **Improve sales mix.** Sell more higher-margin items/less lower-margin items
	Reduce costs and assets 7. **Reduce operating costs.** 8. **Improve asset utilization.**

IDEAS FOR INCREASING UNIT SALES AT THE STRATEGIC ACCOUNT

Use the framework in Figure 6.1 to brainstorm ideas for identifying opportunities for increasing the firm's sales units at the strategic account. Collect your ideas in Figure 6.2.

Figure 6.2: Ideas for Increasing Unit Sales from the Strategic Account

Current Revenue Base	New Revenues
Reduce business lost	**Attract from competitors**
Increase use	**New wallets**

IDEAS FOR IMPROVING MARGINS AND INVESTMENT RETURNS AT THE STRATEGIC ACCOUNT

Use the framework in Figure 6.1 to brainstorm ideas for identifying opportunities for improving margins and investment returns at the strategic account. Collect your ideas in Figure 6.3.

Figure 6.3: Ideas for Improving Margins and Investment Returns at the Strategic Account

Increase Revenues	Improve Efficiency
Improve prices	**Reduce operating costs**
Improve sales mix	**Improve asset utilization**

OPPORTUNITIES LIST

Draw from Figures 6.2 and 6.3 to populate the template in Figure 6.4:

- **Step 1: Select.** Select the top few opportunities from Figures 6.2 and 6.3; place in the left-hand column.

- **Step 2: Forecast revenue potential.** For each selected opportunity, determine potential revenue to your firm.

- **Step 3: Assess chances of success.** Identify the chances that the firm will succeed in this opportunity.

- **Step 4: Required resources.** Identify what resources you need to pursue each opportunity.

- **Step 5: Required actions.** Determine what the firm must do to be successful in this opportunity.

Figure 6.4: Opportunities That You Will Consider Addressing

Opportunity	Revenue Potential	Chances of Success	Required Resources	Required Actions

THREATS

A template for identifying threats is in Figure 6.5:

- **Step 1: Generate ideas.** Brainstorm a list of possible threats; write these in the left-hand column.

- **Step 2: Threat potential.** For each threat, assess how much revenue is at risk.

- **Step 3: Nature of the threat.** Describe the type of threat.

- **Step 4: Likelihood threat will succeed.** Assess the chances of the threat succeeding.

- **Step 5: Possible action.** What actions could the firm take to repel each threat?

Figure 6.5: Threats

Threat	Threat Potential	Nature of the Threat	Likelihood Threat Will Succeed	Possible Action

PART 4

STRATEGY AND IMPLEMENTATION

AT THIS STAGE IN THE STRATEGIC ACCOUNT PLANNING PROCESS, you have completed the *situation analysis*, developed *planning assumptions*, and identified *opportunities and threats* for the firm at the strategic account. Now you are ready to lay out the strategic account strategy and action programs according to the framework discussed in Chapter 1.

CHAPTER 7

The Strategic Account Strategy

THE TEMPLATE FOR LAYING OUT THE STRATEGIC ACCOUNT STRATEGY IS IN FIGURE 7.1. This figure documents how you intend to approach the strategic account. Chapter 8 focuses on the specific action programs that you will implement. The strategic account strategy must contain the following elements:

VISION

Describe your aspirations for the strategic account. Where would you like to lead your strategic account team with regard to this account? How would you like this account to see you, your team, and your business?

MISSION

Describe from where, specifically, you will derive revenues. What products and/or services will you sell to which business units within your account? And in which geographies?

PERFORMANCE OBJECTIVES

Describe what your firm intends to achieve at the strategic account:

- **Strategic objectives:** Directional — will you grow revenue, share, profitability, or cash flow?

- **Operational objectives:** Specific numbers and time frames.

STRATEGIC FOCUS

Describe how you intend to improve the profitability of your business at the account. The strategic focus should relate to the type of opportunities and threats you identified in Chapter 6:

- Protecting/maintaining your share of the account's current wallets

- Growing your share of the account's current wallets

- Helping the strategic account to grow its revenues (in its current business)

- Growing your share of the account's overall spend by increasing the size of the wallet that would be spent with you at the expense of your competitors

- Helping the strategic account to grow its revenues by finding new business opportunities

- Finding ways to offer new value-added services to the strategic account

- Increasing prices

- Changing the sales mix to emphasize higher-margin offerings

- Reducing the cost of selling and servicing the account

- Improving asset utilization at the account.

POSITIONING STATEMENT

The positioning statement should comprise these elements:

- **Customer targets.** Which individuals at the strategic account do you have to convince to do business with your firm?

- **Competitive targets.** Who are you going up against at the strategic account?

- **Value proposition.** What value are you offering the customer targets?

- **Reason to believe.** Why should the target customers believe you can deliver the value you promise in the value proposition?

Figure 7.1: Strategic Account Strategy

Strategic Account:	Strategic Account Manager:	Time Frame:

Vision *Aspirational*		
Mission *Specifically where we will seek revenues*		
Objectives	**Strategic** *Directional*	
	Operational *Numbers and time frame*	
Strategic Focus		
Positioning	**Customer targets**	
	Competitor targets	
	Value proposition	
	Reason to believe	

CHAPTER 8

Action at the
Strategic Account

THE STRATEGIC ACCOUNT STRATEGY GIVES RISE TO TWO SORTS OF ACTION PROGRAMS — *strategic* action programs and *relationship-building* action programs.

INDIVIDUAL ACTION PROGRAMS

STRATEGIC ACTION PROGRAMS

The template for laying out a *strategic* action program is in Figure 8.1. This figure documents:

- **Objectives.** What are the objectives of the action programs?

- **Action steps.** List the steps required to achieve the objectives, including answers to *who, what, how, when* questions.

- **Force field analysis.** Perform a force field analysis for each action program and answer the following questions:
  - What are the enabling forces?
  - What are the resisting forces?
  - How can we enhance the enabling forces?
  - How can we redirect or diminish the resisting forces?

RELATIONSHIP-BUILDING ACTION PROGRAMS

The template for laying out a *relationship-building* action program is in Figure 8.2. This figure documents:

- **Objectives.** What are the objectives of the action programs?

- **Action steps.** List the steps required to achieve the objectives, including answers to the *who, what, how, when* questions.

- **Force field analysis.** Perform a force field analysis for each action program and answer the following questions:
  - What are the enabling forces?
  - What are the resisting forces?
  - How can we enhance the enabling forces?
  - How can we redirect or diminish the resisting forces?

Figure 8.1: Strategic Action Programs

Action program				
Objective				
Action steps				
Who?				
What?				
How?				
When?				
Enabling forces/ resisting forces				

Note: Duplicate Figure 8.1 as many times as you need to cover all strategic action programs.

Figure 8.2: Relationship-Building Action Program

Target individual				
Objective				
Action steps				
Who?				
What?				
How?				
When?				
Enabling forces/ resisting forces				

Note: Duplicate Figure 8.2 as many times as you need to cover all the relationship-building programs.

THE SET OF STRATEGIC ACTION PROGRAMS

If the strategic account manager develops several action programs in the strategic account's various business units, it is often useful to present the entire set together. Such a presentation allows the firm to assess if it is overstretching its own and/or the strategic account's resources.

Figure 8.3 illustrates a set of strategic account programs. It shows that the firm has an action program of type 3 in four different business units at the strategic account — C, D, E, and F. Question: Does the firm have the resources to conduct all of these action programs simultaneously?

Figure 8.3: Illustration of a Set of Strategic Action Programs

Type of Firm Action Program

	1	2	3	4	5	6	7	8
A	X							
B		X						
C			X	X	X	X	X	X
D			X					
E			X					
F			X					
G		X		X			X	
H	X			X				

Figure 8.3 also shows that the firm has six different types of action program — 3, 4, 5, 6, 7, 8, in customer business unit C. Question: Does the customer have the capacity to support each of these action programs?

Figure 8.4 provides a template for developing a set of strategic actino programs.

Figure 8.4: Set of Strategic Action Programs

Type of Firm Action Program

	1	2	3	4	5	6	7	8
A								
B								
C								
D								
E								
F								
G								
H								

www.ingramcontent.com/pod-product-compliance
Lightning Source LLC
Chambersburg PA
CBHW081513200326
41518CB00015B/2489